Compositions
for Guitar

Matthew Leigh EMBLETON (b1978)

Copyright ©2020 Matthew Leigh Embleton. All rights reserved.

Compositions for Guitar

01 Journey in d-minor 4
02 Nocturnes in d-minor and e-minor 6
03 From Depth in a-minor 8
04 Nocturnes in f-minor and g-minor 9
05 Small Floating Crafts in c-minor 12
06 Journey in a-minor 16
07 Journey in c-minor 20
08 Nocturne in c-minor 24
09 Tasmanian Lake d-minor 26
10 Extransience in d-minor 27
11 Victoria Park, December 2005 in e-minor (Version 1) 28
11 Victoria Park, December 2005 in e-minor (Version 2) 29
12 Late Night Sky in g-minor 30
13 Introduction in g-minor 31

Acknowledgments

Thanks to Osamu Yano for your collaboration, feedback, support, encouragement, friendship, and your fantastic recordings.

Thanks to the special people in my life who have supported and encouraged me in my work. Thank you for believing in me. You know who you are.

Matthew Leigh Embleton (b1978) Compositions for Guitar

Op 01 Journey in d-minor

01 Introduction, *piano con affetto*

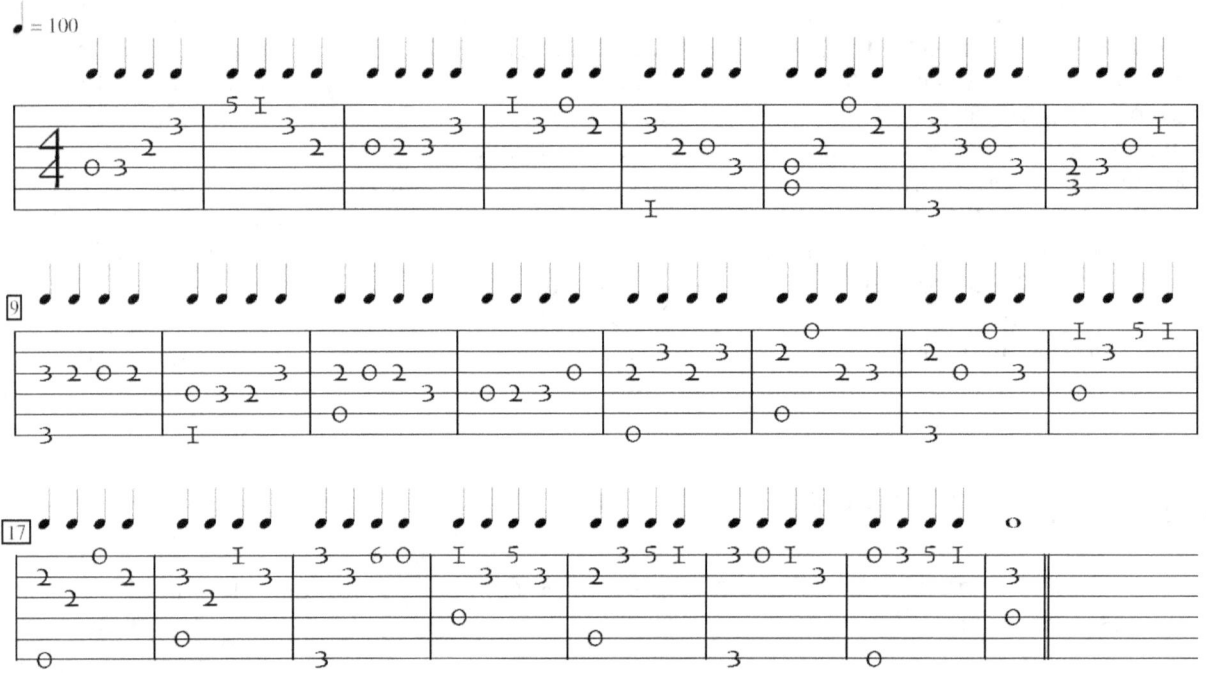

02 The Pursuit, *con affetto e un poco agitato*

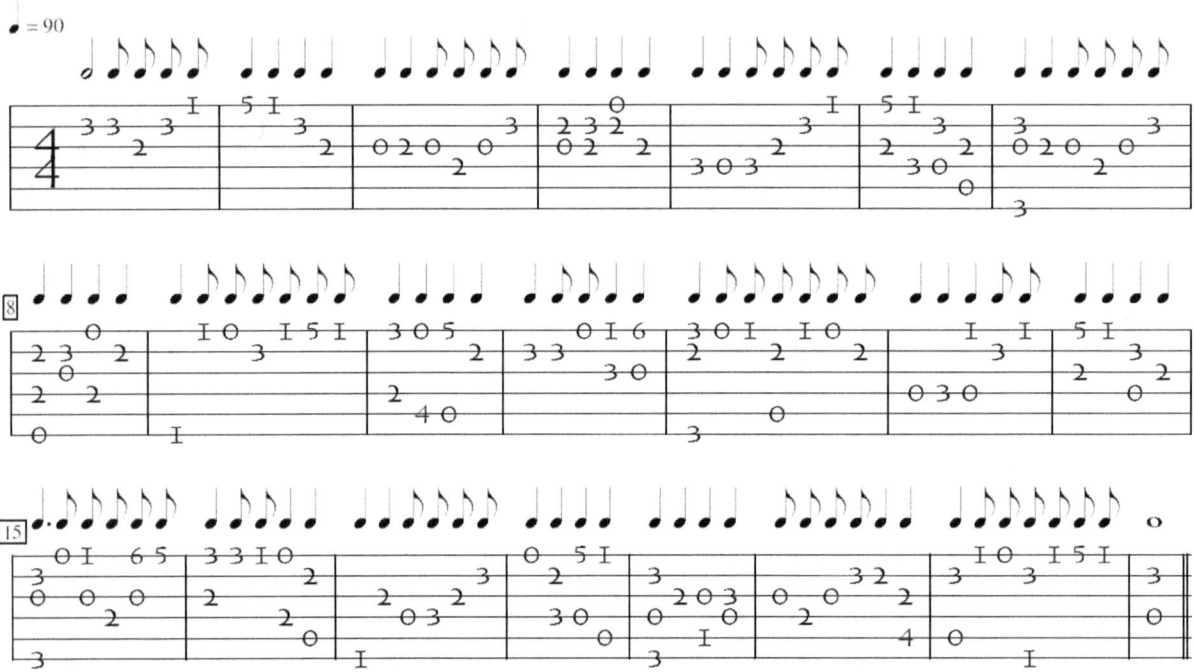

©2012, 2013, 2015, and 2020 Matthew Leigh Embleton

Matthew Leigh Embleton (b1978) — Compositions for Guitar

03 Looking Skyward, *con larghezza*

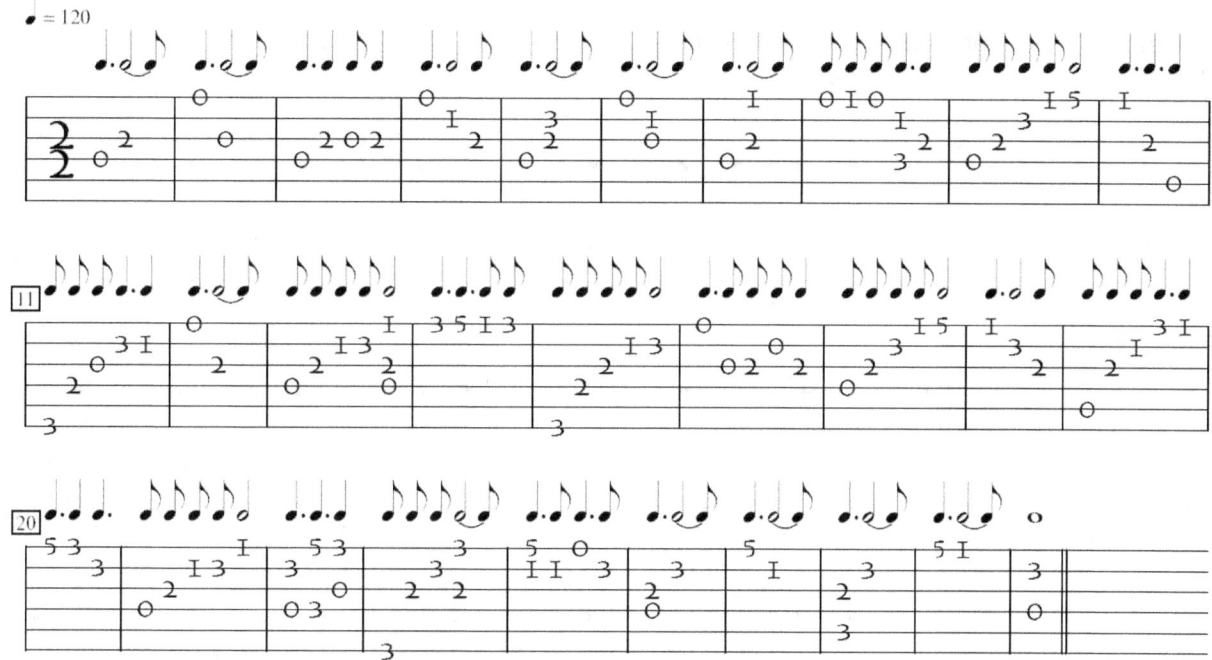

©2012, 2013, 2015, and 2020 Matthew Leigh Embleton

Matthew Leigh Embleton (b1978) — Compositions for Guitar

Op 02 Nocturnes in d-minor and e-minor

01 Nocturne in d-minor, *piano molto e cantabile*

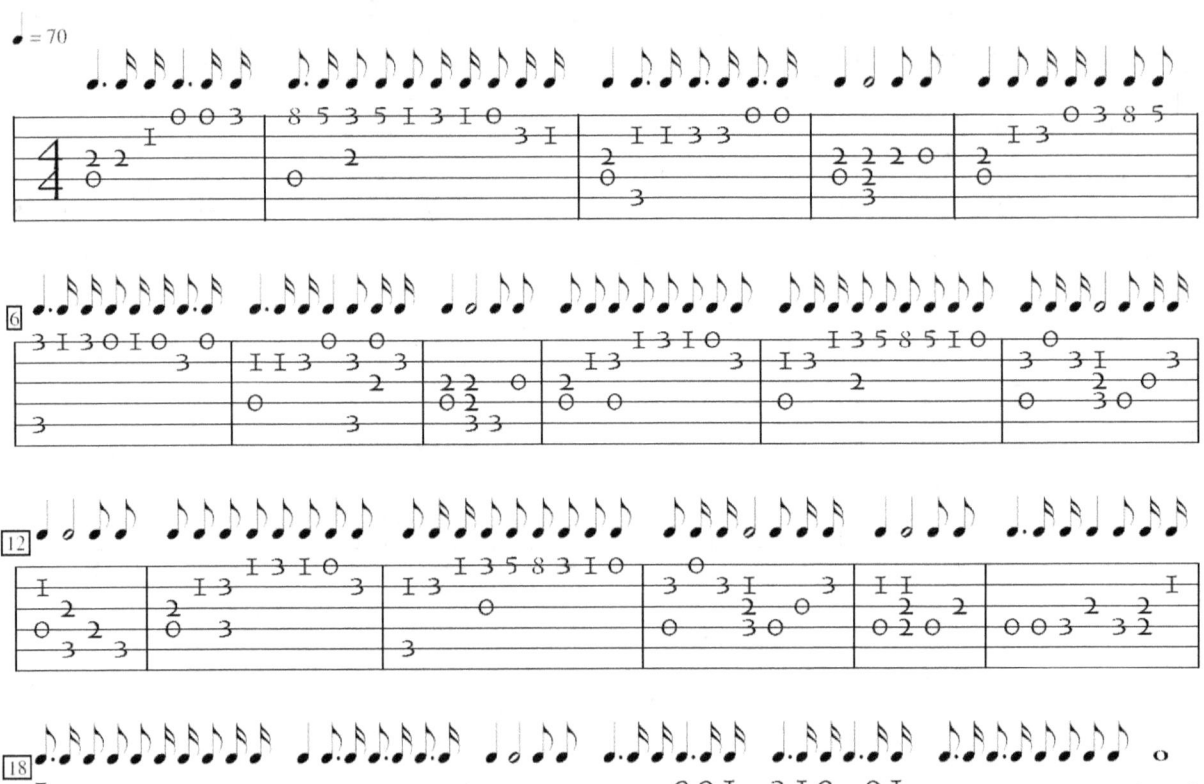

©2012, 2013, 2015, and 2020 Matthew Leigh Embleton

Matthew Leigh Embleton (b1978) — Compositions for Guitar

02 Nocturne in e-minor, *piano molto e cantabile*

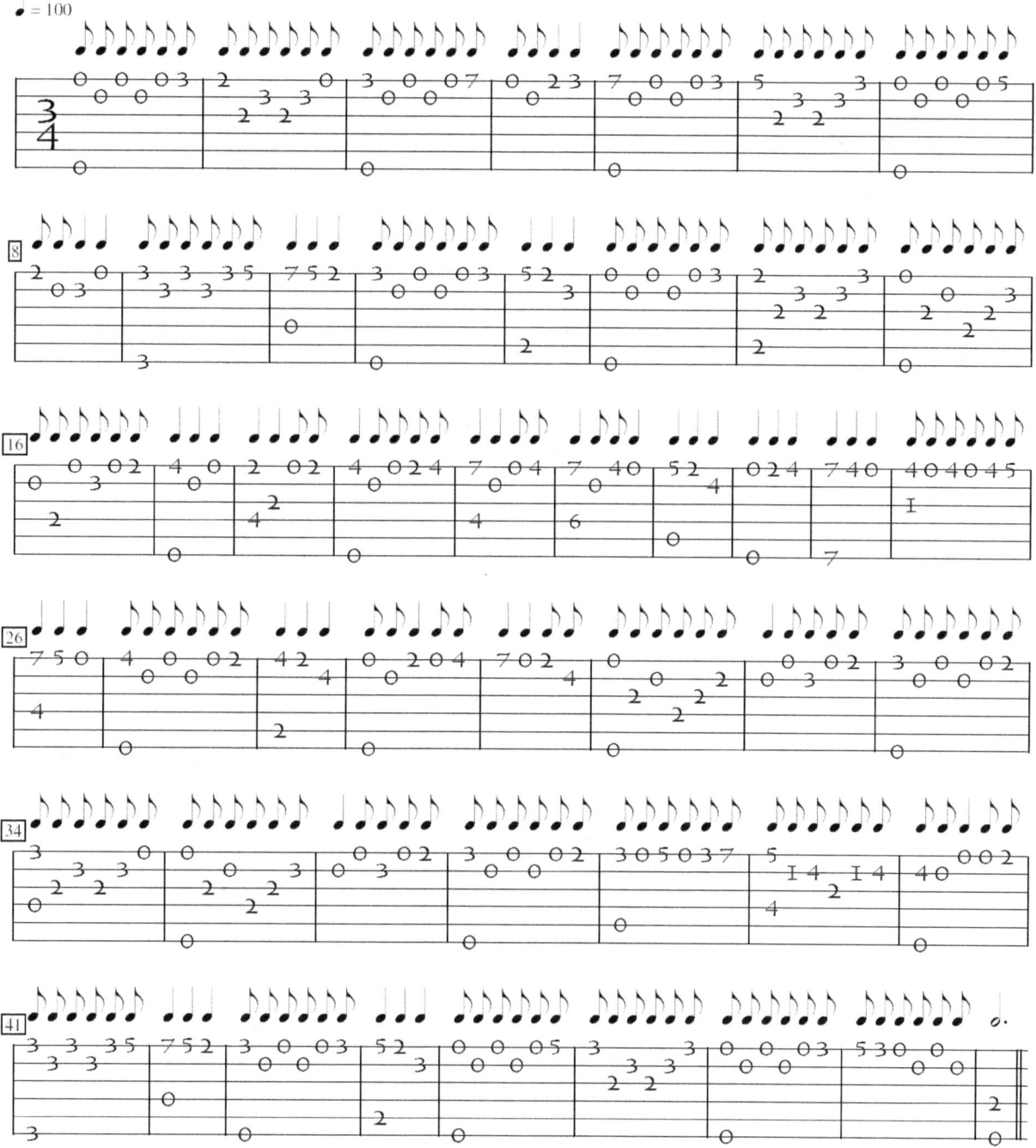

Matthew Leigh Embleton (b1978)   Compositions for Guitar

Op 03 From Depth in a-minor

Piano molto e penseroso

©2012, 2013, 2015, and 2020 Matthew Leigh Embleton

Matthew Leigh Embleton (b1978) Compositions for Guitar

Op 04 Nocturnes in f-minor and g-minor

01 Nocturne in f-minor, *piano molto e cantabile (Capo 1st Fret)*

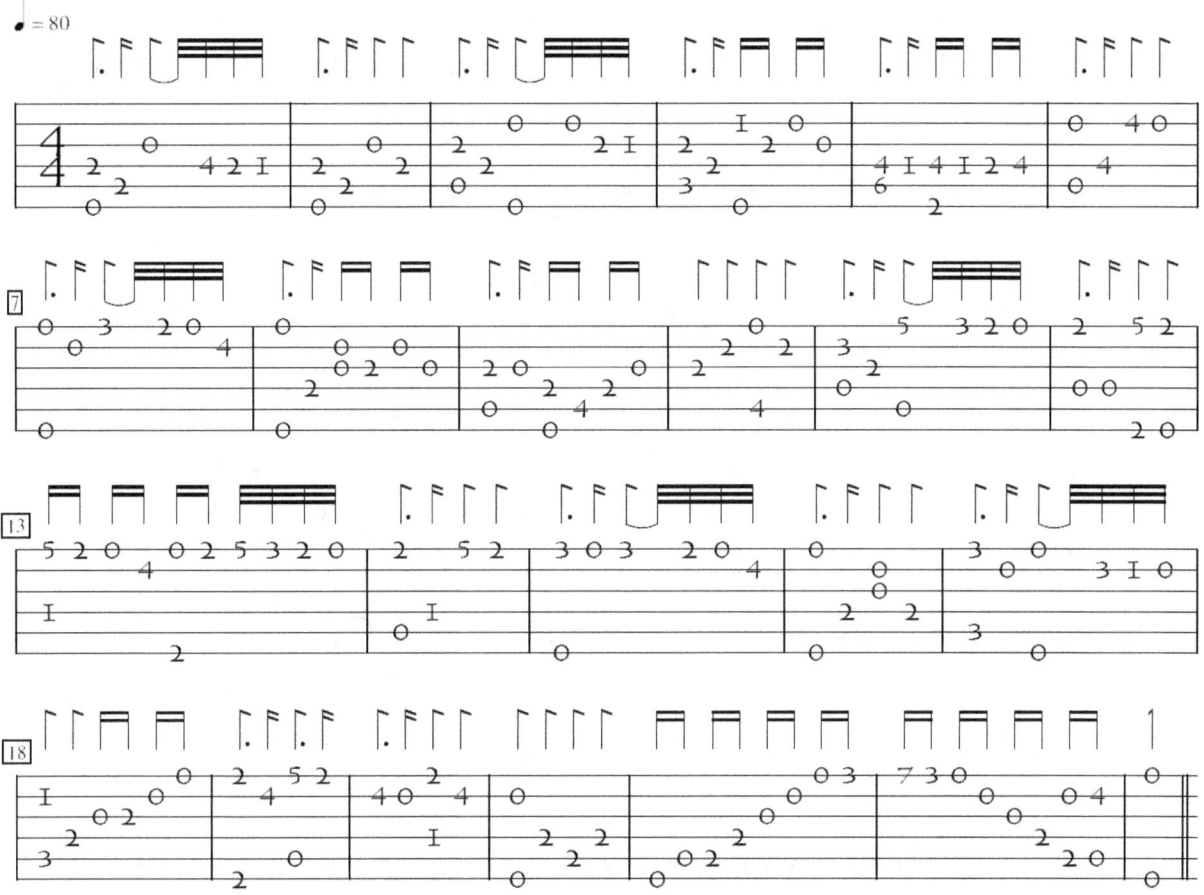

©2012, 2013, 2015, and 2020 Matthew Leigh Embleton

Matthew Leigh Embleton (b1978) — Compositions for Guitar

02 Nocturne in g-minor (Version 1), *piano molto e cantabile*

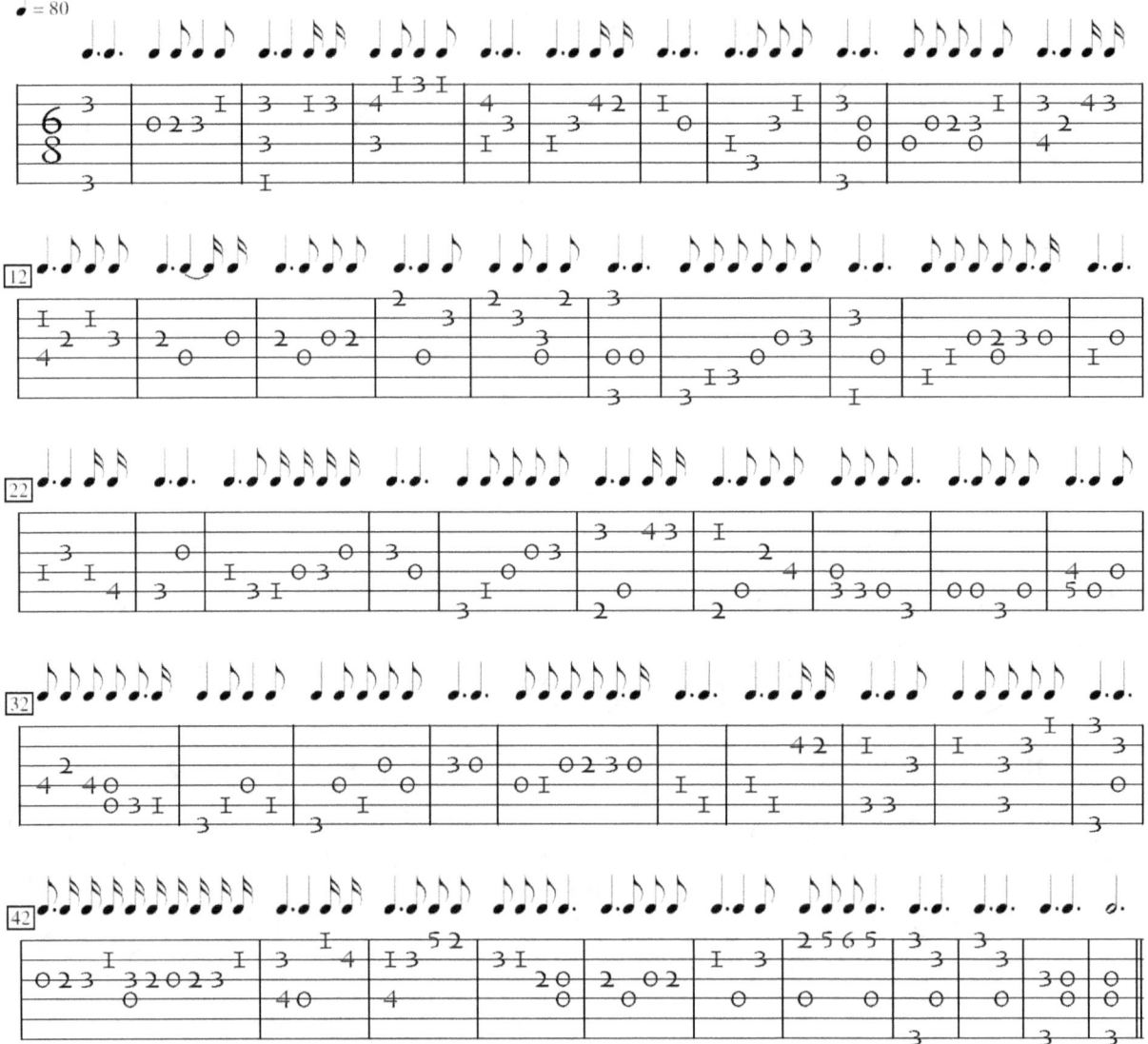

©2012, 2013, 2015, and 2020 Matthew Leigh Embleton

Matthew Leigh Embleton (b1978) — Compositions for Guitar

02 Nocturne in g-minor (Version 2), *piano molto e cantabile*

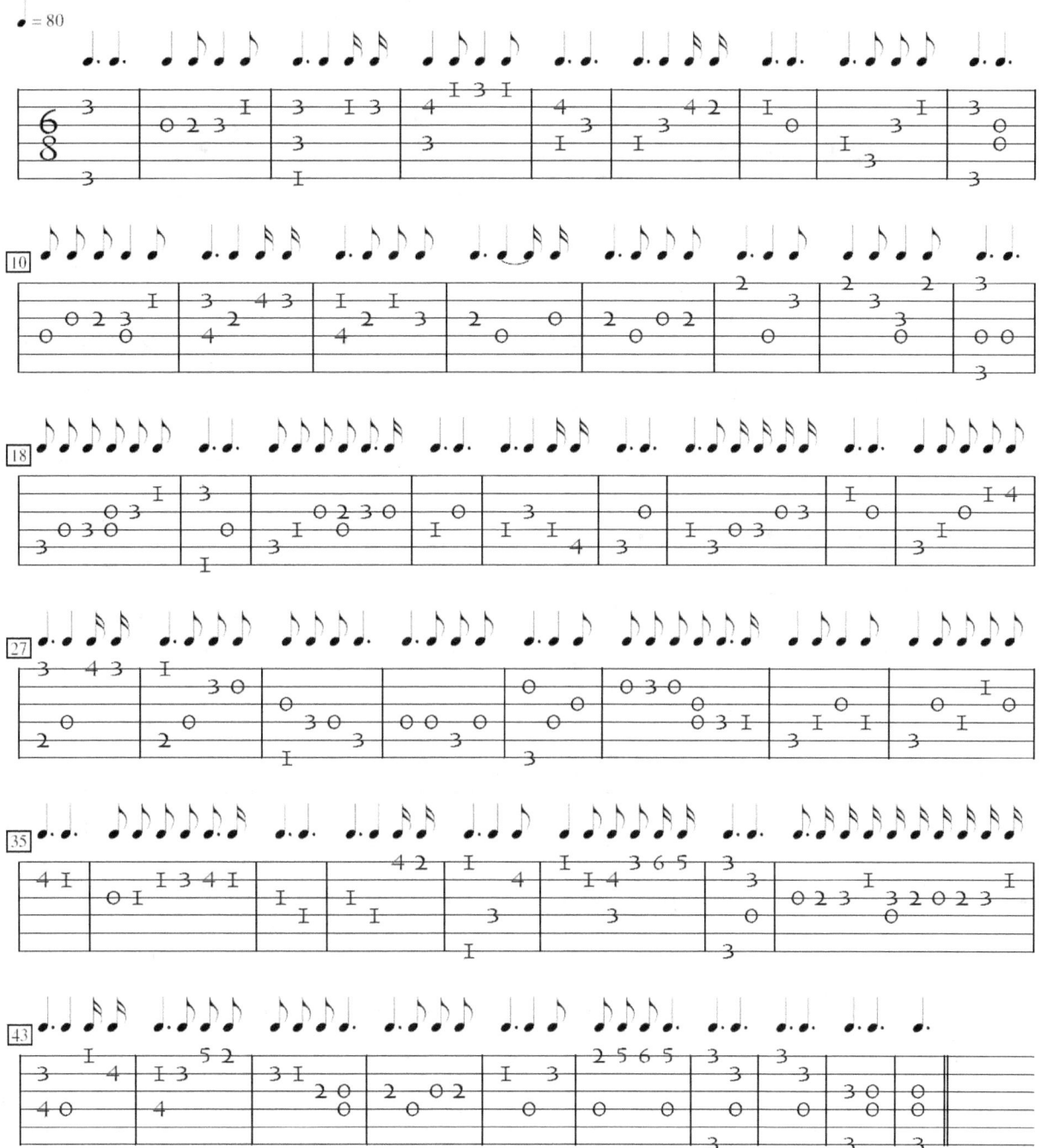

Op 05 Small Floating Crafts in c-minor

01 Introduction, *con rubato e improvvisazione (Capo 3rd Fret)*

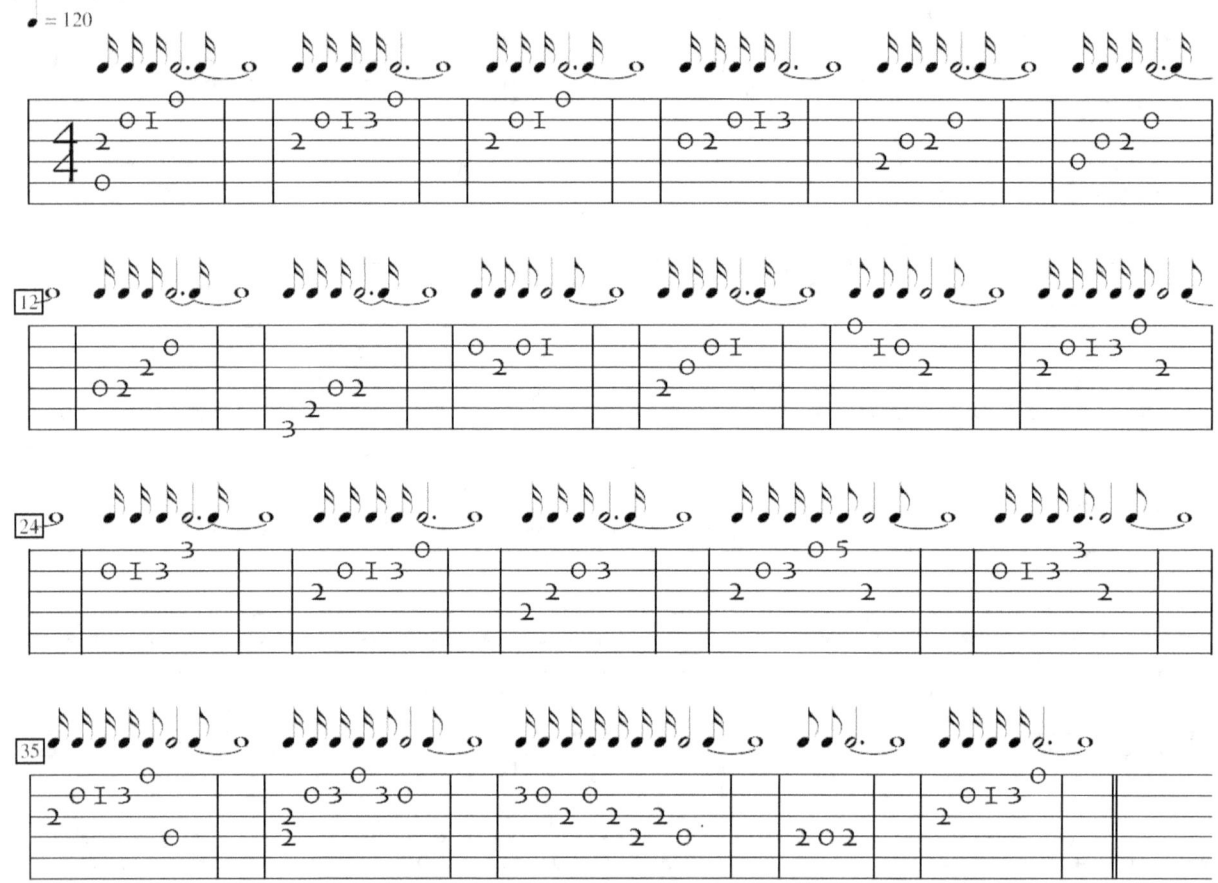

02 Interlude, *con rubato e improvvisazione (Capo 3rd Fret)*

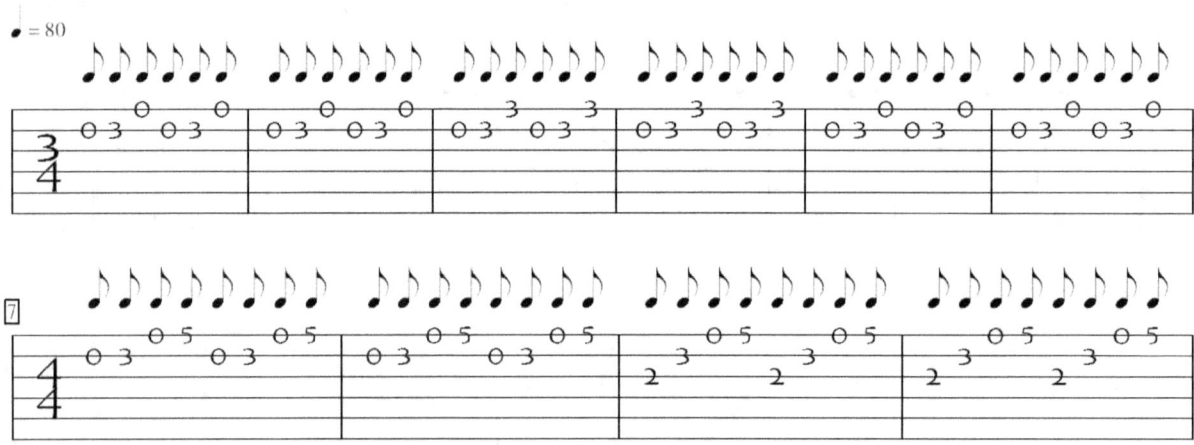

Matthew Leigh Embleton (b1978) — Compositions for Guitar

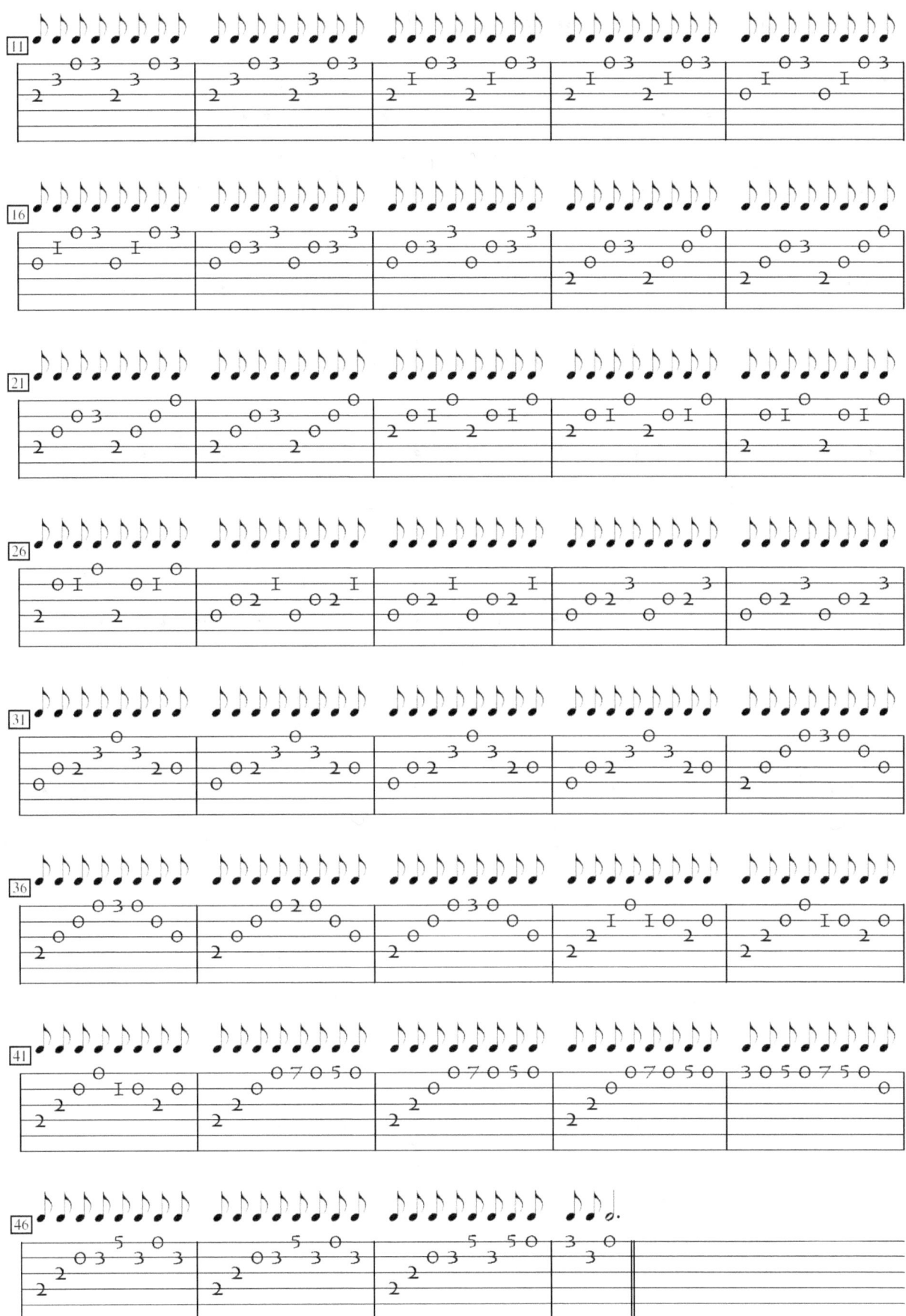

©2012, 2013, 2015, and 2020 Matthew Leigh Embleton

Matthew Leigh Embleton (b1978) — Compositions for Guitar

03 Conclusion, *con rubato e improvvisazione (Capo 3rd Fret)*

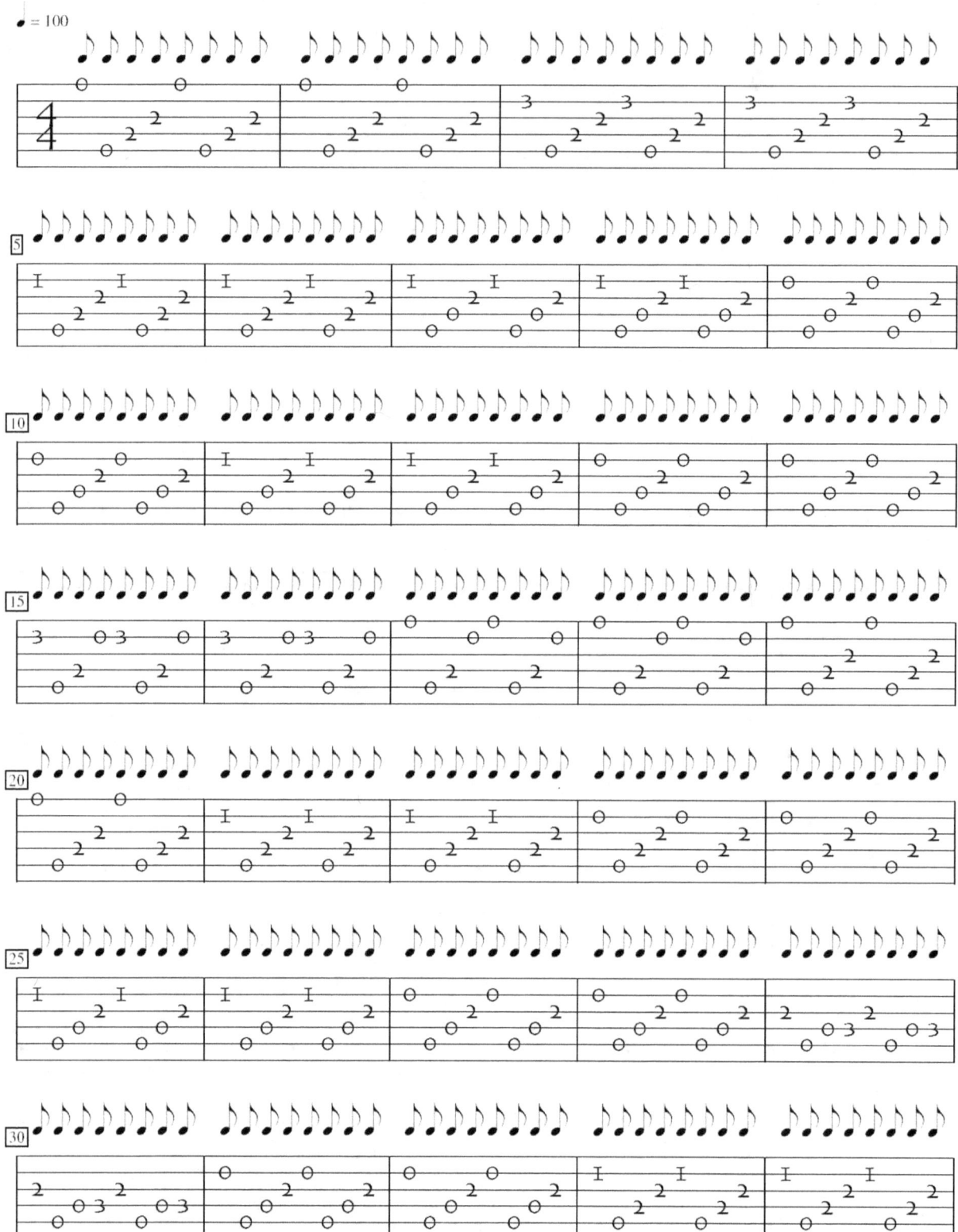

©2012, 2013, 2015, and 2020 Matthew Leigh Embleton

Matthew Leigh Embleton (b1978) — Compositions for Guitar

©2012, 2013, 2015, and 2020 Matthew Leigh Embleton

Matthew Leigh Embleton (b1978) — Compositions for Guitar

Op 06 Journey in a-minor

01 Arpeggiata, *adagio andante e piano*

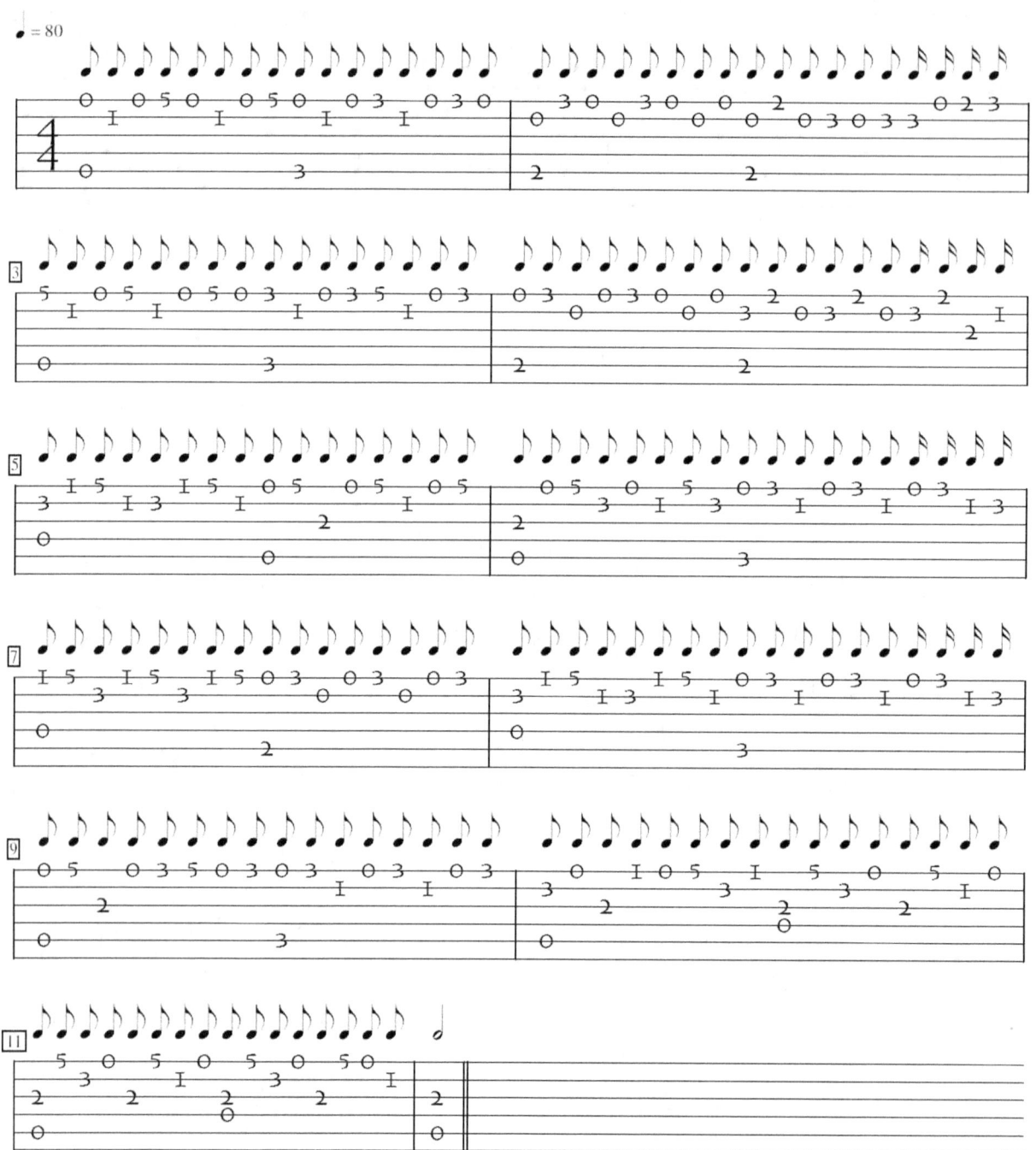

©2012, 2013, 2015, and 2020 Matthew Leigh Embleton

Matthew Leigh Embleton (b1978) Compositions for Guitar

02 Cloud Level (Version 1), *piano molto e penseroso*

02 Cloud Level (Version 2), *piano molto e penseroso*

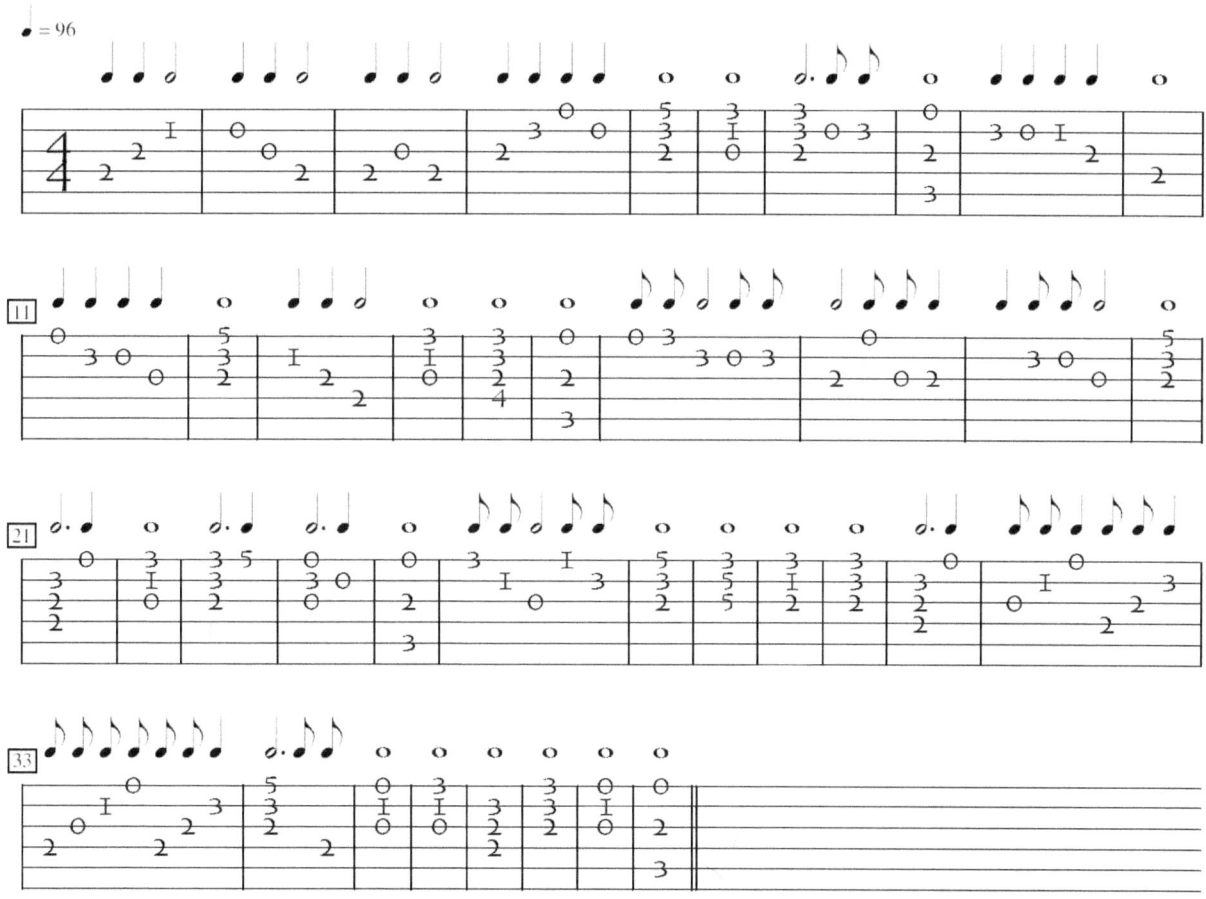

©2012, 2013, 2015, and 2020 Matthew Leigh Embleton

Compositions for Guitar

Matthew Leigh Embleton (b1978)

03 Eternal Recurrence, *piano molto con affetuoso*

©2012, 2013, 2015, and 2020 Matthew Leigh Embleton

Matthew Leigh Embleton (b1978)   Compositions for Guitar

Op 07 Journey in c-minor

01 Introduction, *andante (Capo 3rd Fret)*

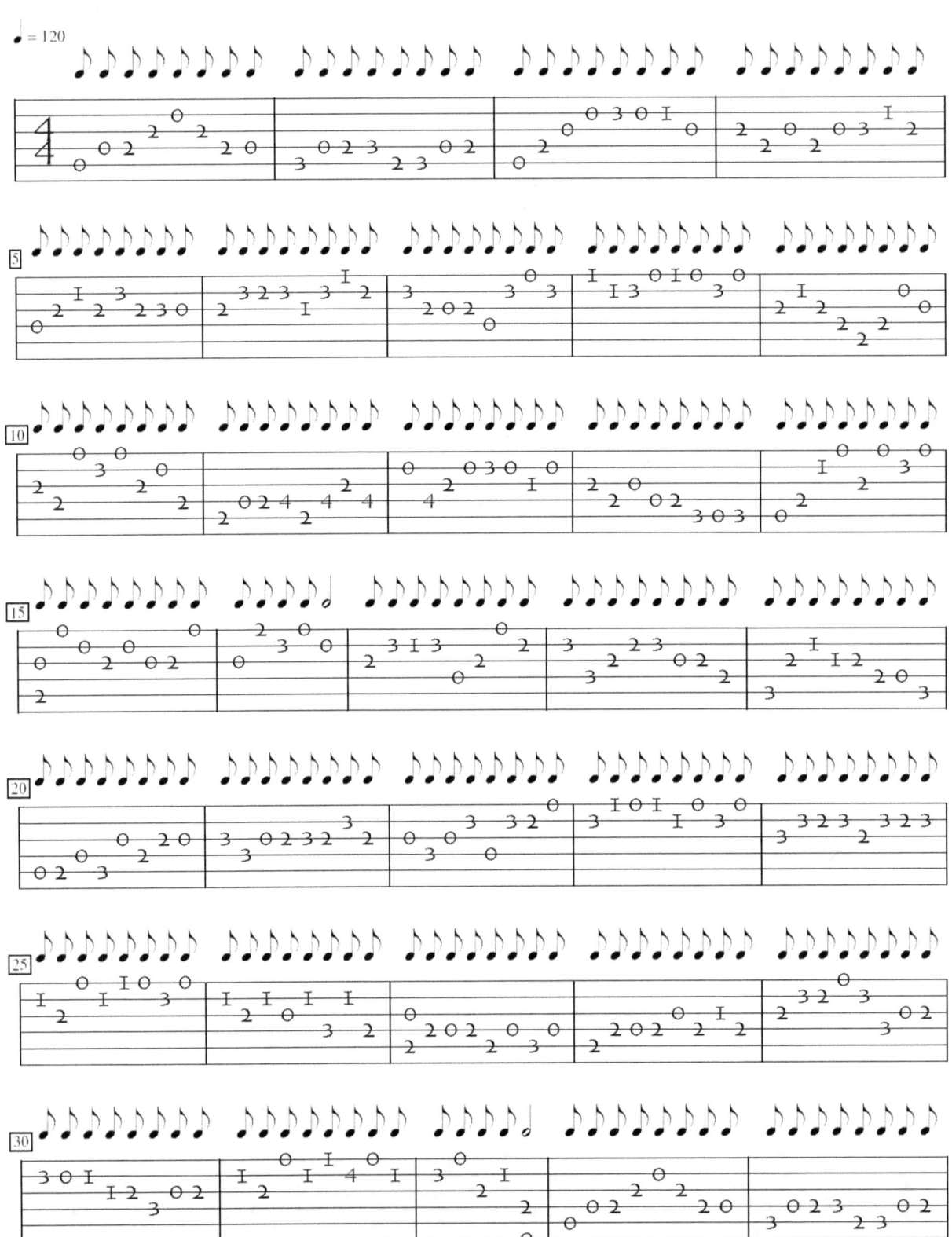

©2012, 2013, 2015, and 2020 Matthew Leigh Embleton

Matthew Leigh Embleton (b1978) — Compositions for Guitar

©2012, 2013, 2015, and 2020 Matthew Leigh Embleton

Matthew Leigh Embleton (b1978)   Compositions for Guitar

02 Interlude, *adagio (Capo 3rd Fret)*

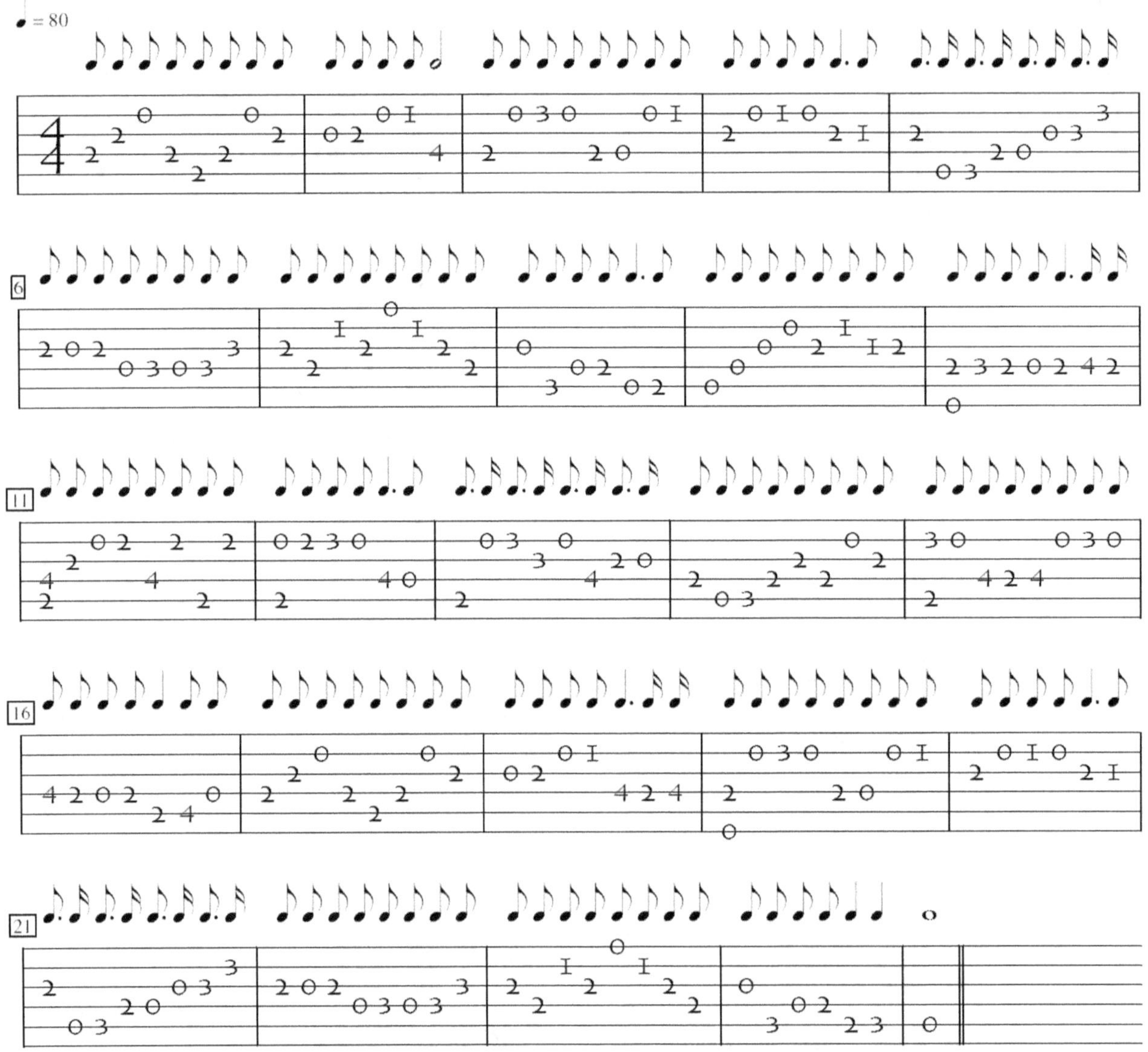

03 Conclusion, *allegro (Capo 3rd Fret)*

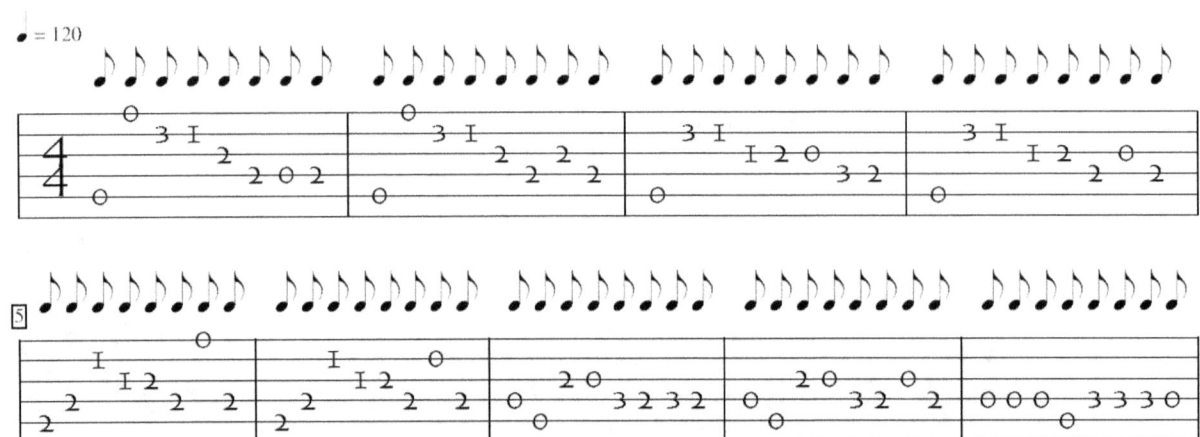

©2012, 2013, 2015, and 2020 Matthew Leigh Embleton

Matthew Leigh Embleton (b1978) — Compositions for Guitar

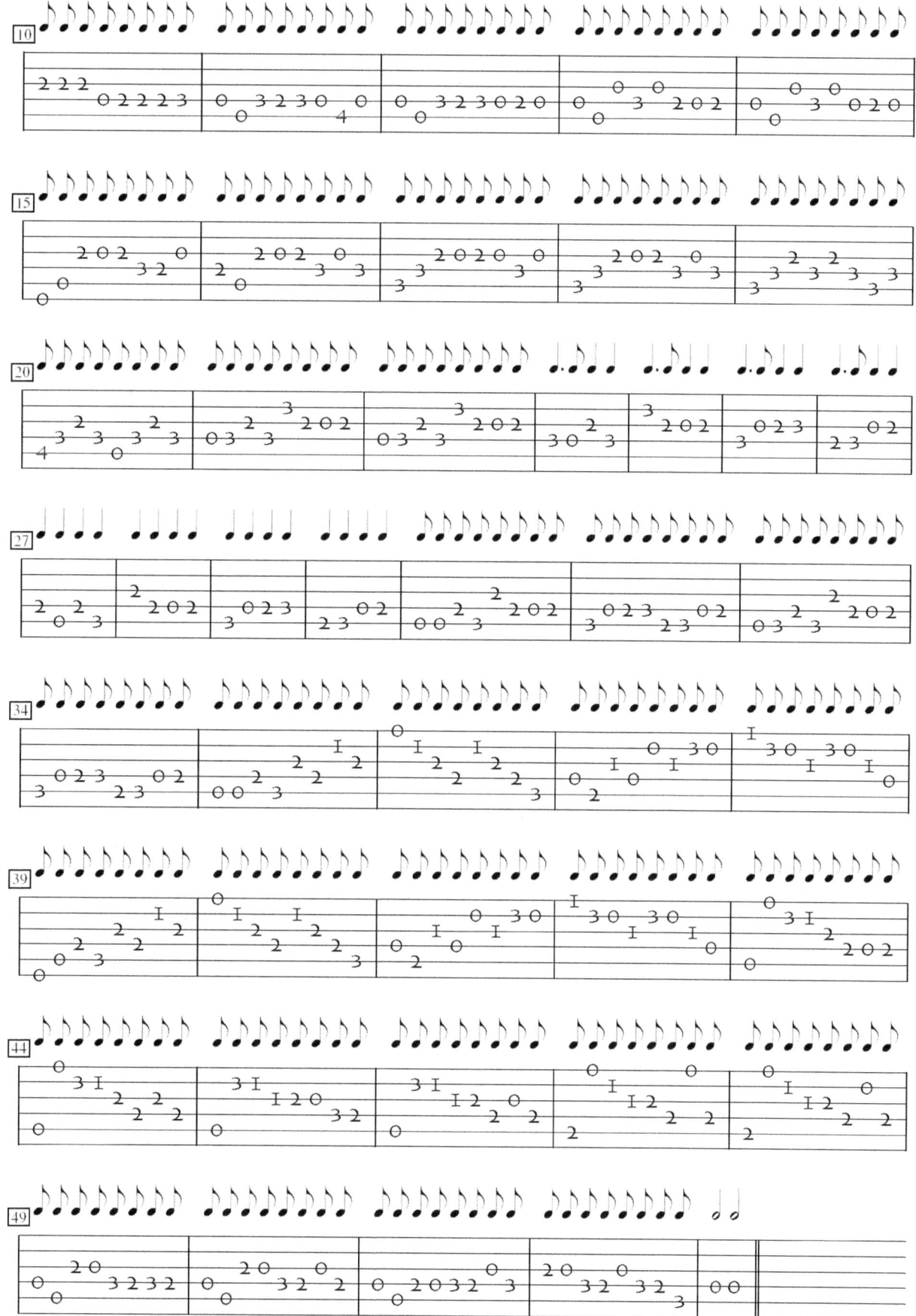

©2012, 2013, 2015, and 2020 Matthew Leigh Embleton

Matthew Leigh Embleton (b1978) Compositions for Guitar

Op 08 Nocturne in c-minor

Piano molto e cantabile (Capo 3rd Fret)

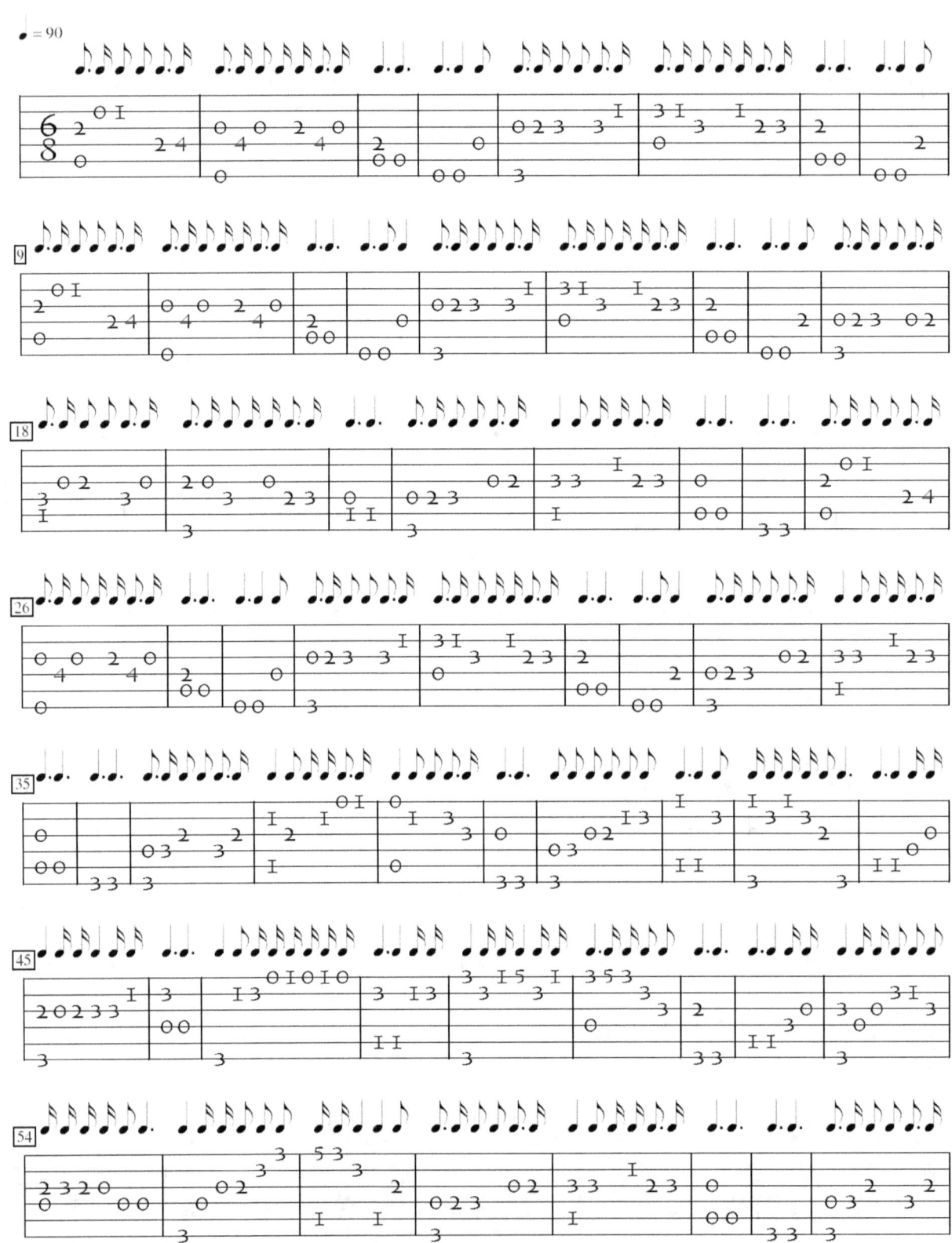

©2012, 2013, 2015, and 2020 Matthew Leigh Embleton

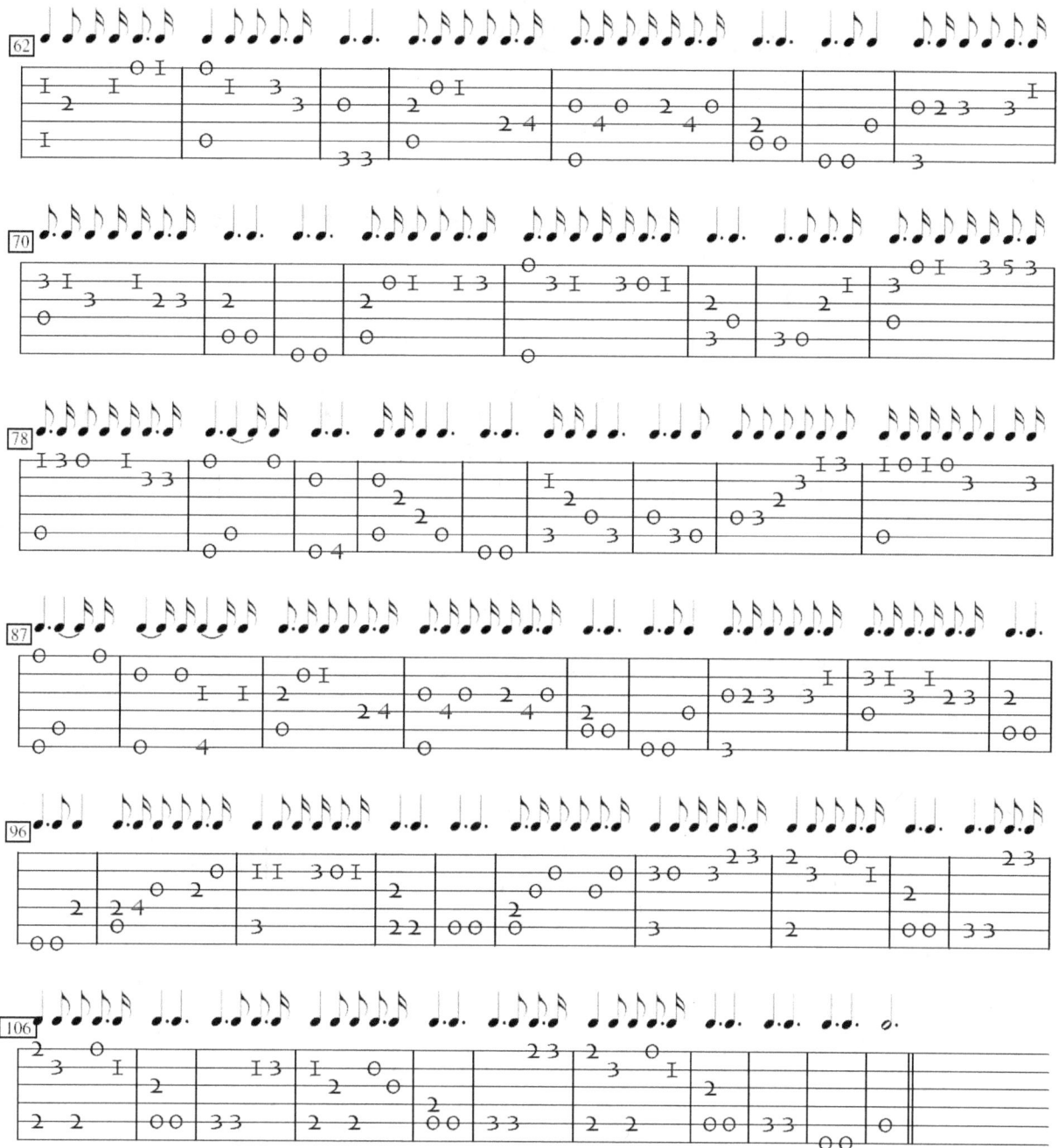

Matthew Leigh Embleton (b1978) Compositions for Guitar

Op 09 Tasmanian Lake d-minor

Piano molto e penseroso

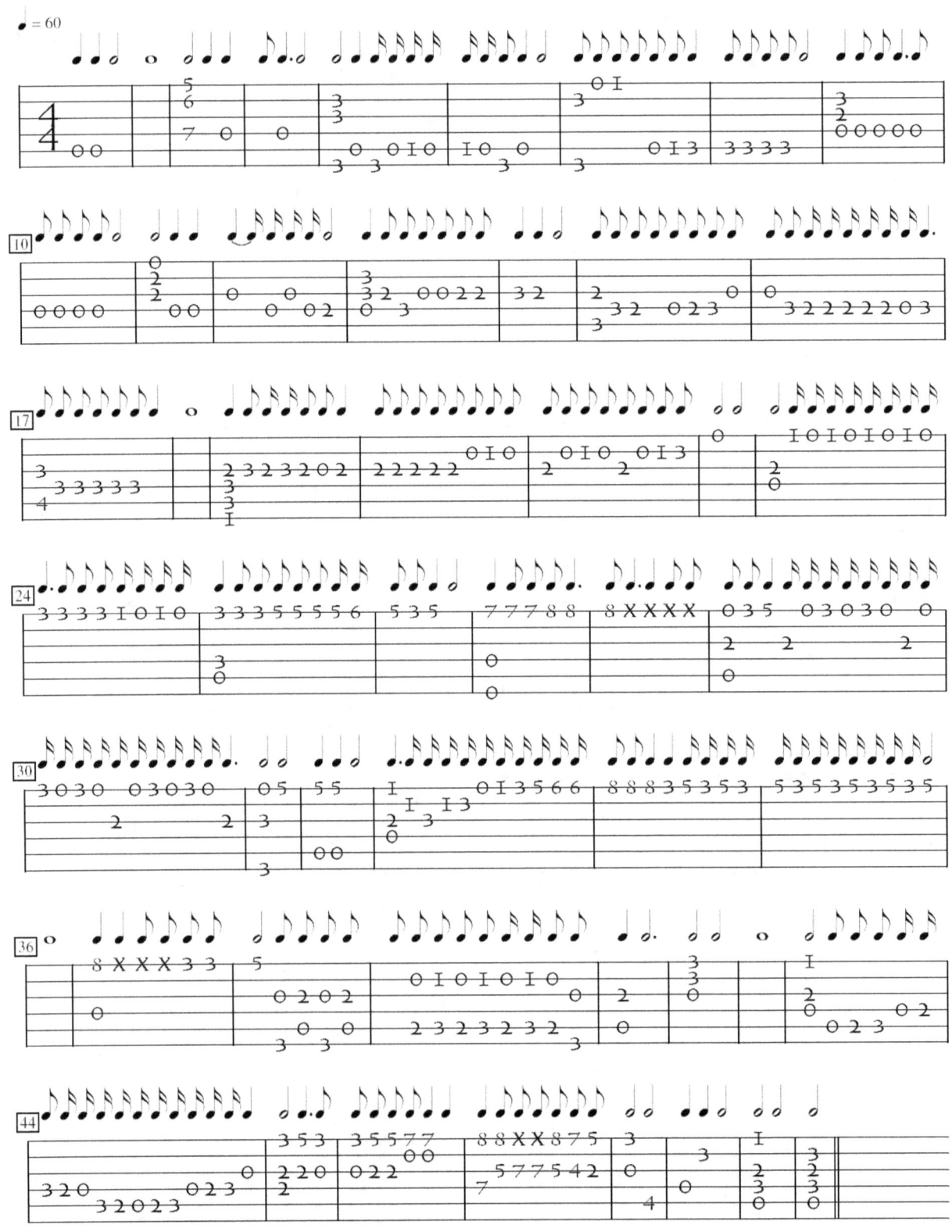

©2012, 2013, 2015, and 2020 Matthew Leigh Embleton

Matthew Leigh Embleton (b1978) — Compositions for Guitar

Op 10 Extransience in d-minor

Affrettando con poco agitato

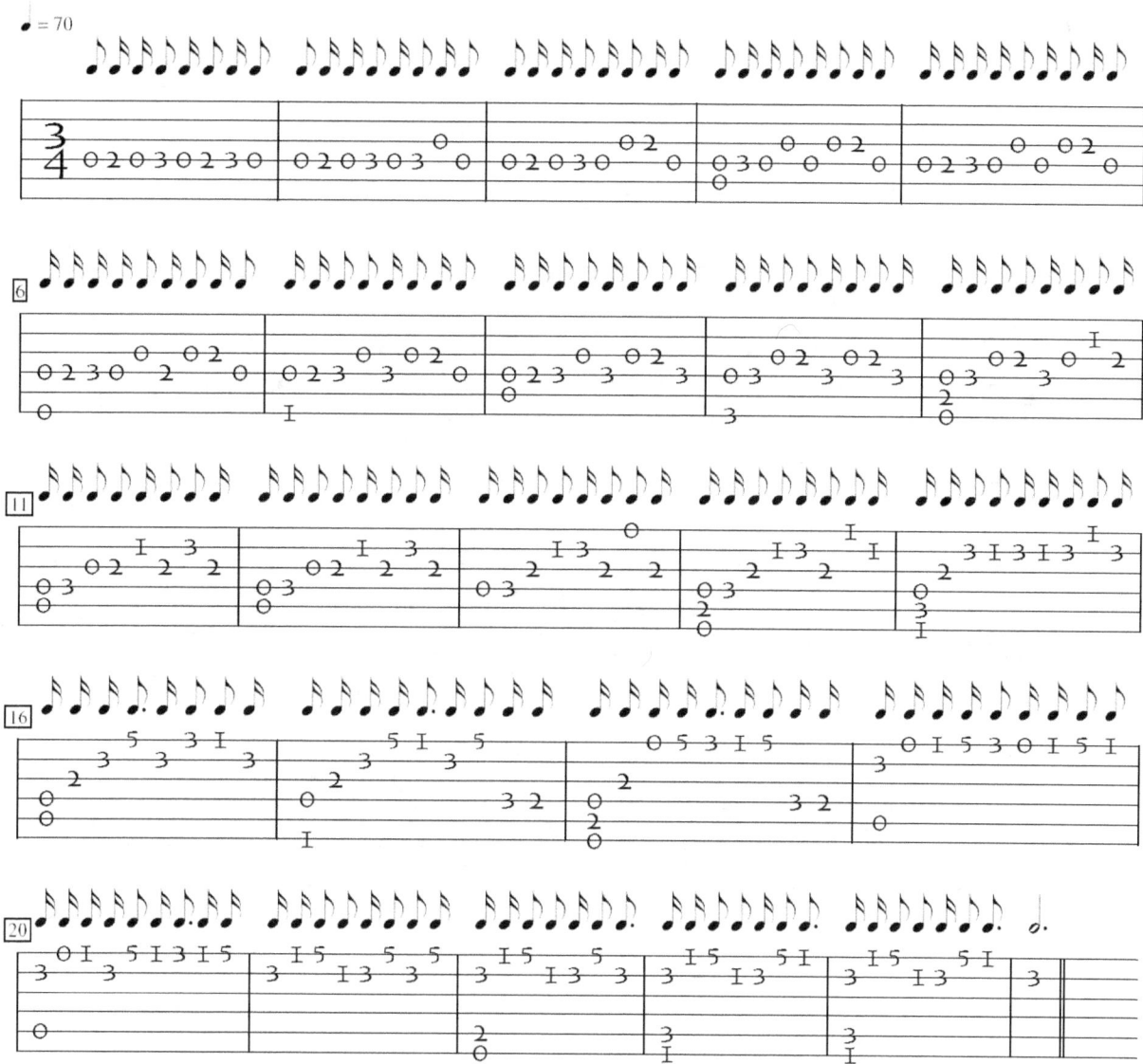

©2012, 2013, 2015, and 2020 Matthew Leigh Embleton

Op 11 Victoria Park, December 2005 in e-minor (Version 1)

Piano molto e penseroso

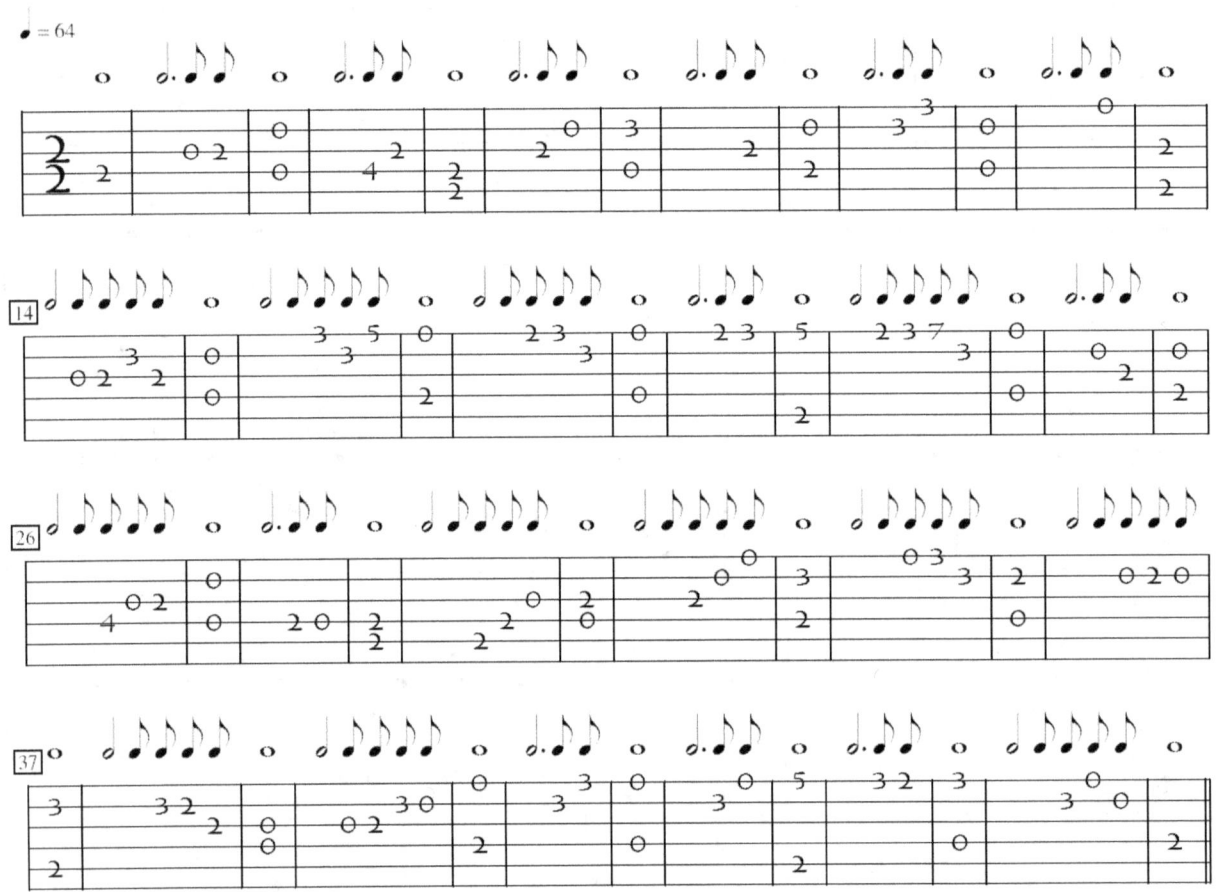

Op 11 Victoria Park, December 2005 in e-minor (Version 2)

Piano molto e penseroso

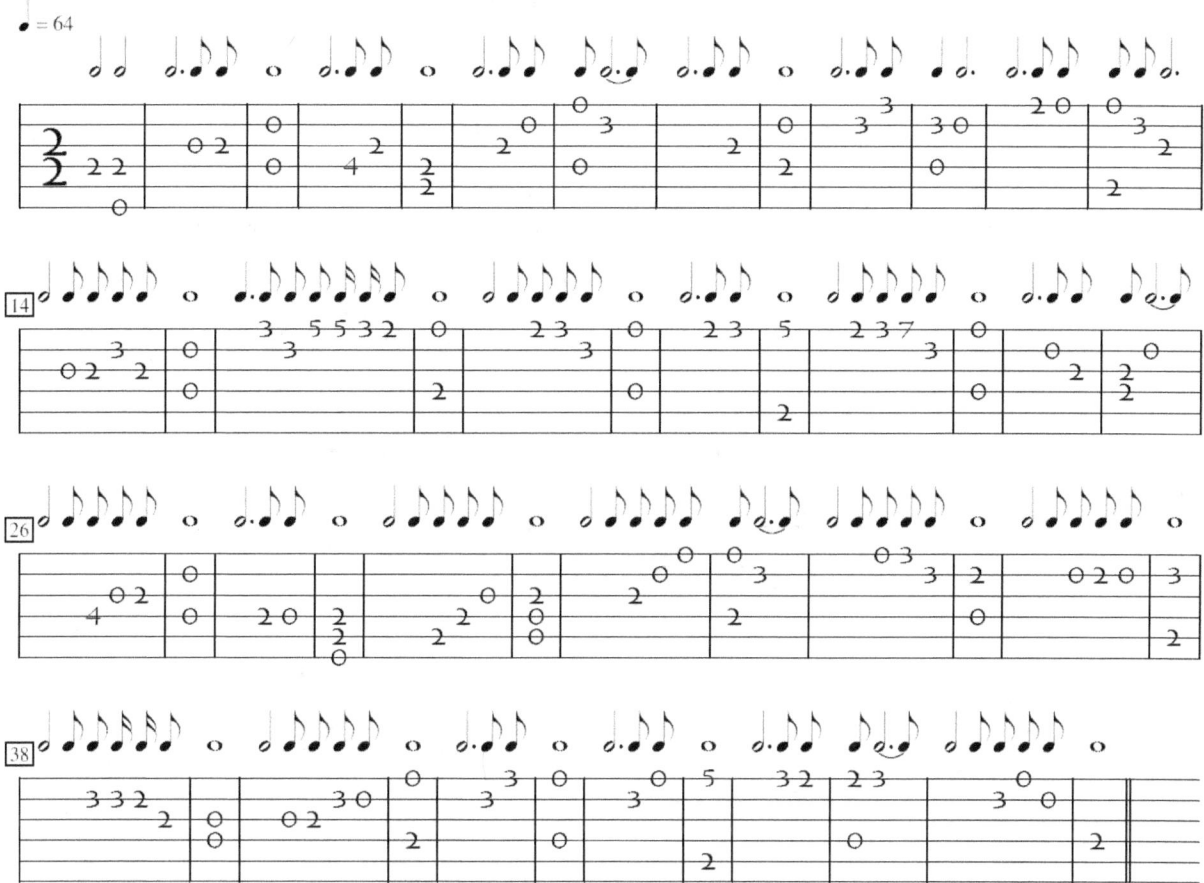

Matthew Leigh Embleton (b1978) — Compositions for Guitar

Op 12 Late Night Sky in g-minor

Piano molto e penseroso

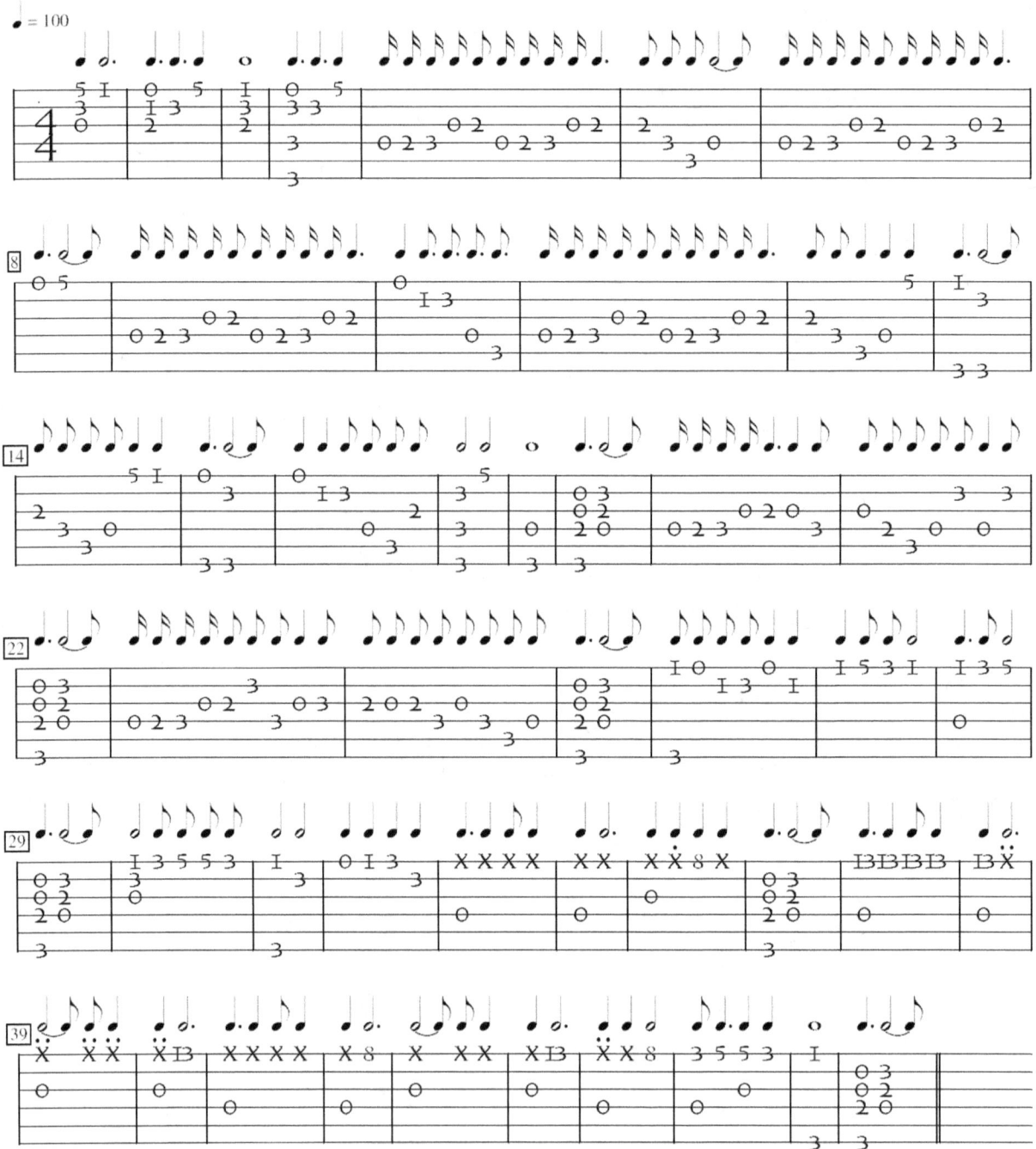

©2012, 2013, 2015, and 2020 Matthew Leigh Embleton

Matthew Leigh Embleton (b1978) — Compositions for Guitar

Op 13 Introduction in g-minor

Piano molto e cantabile

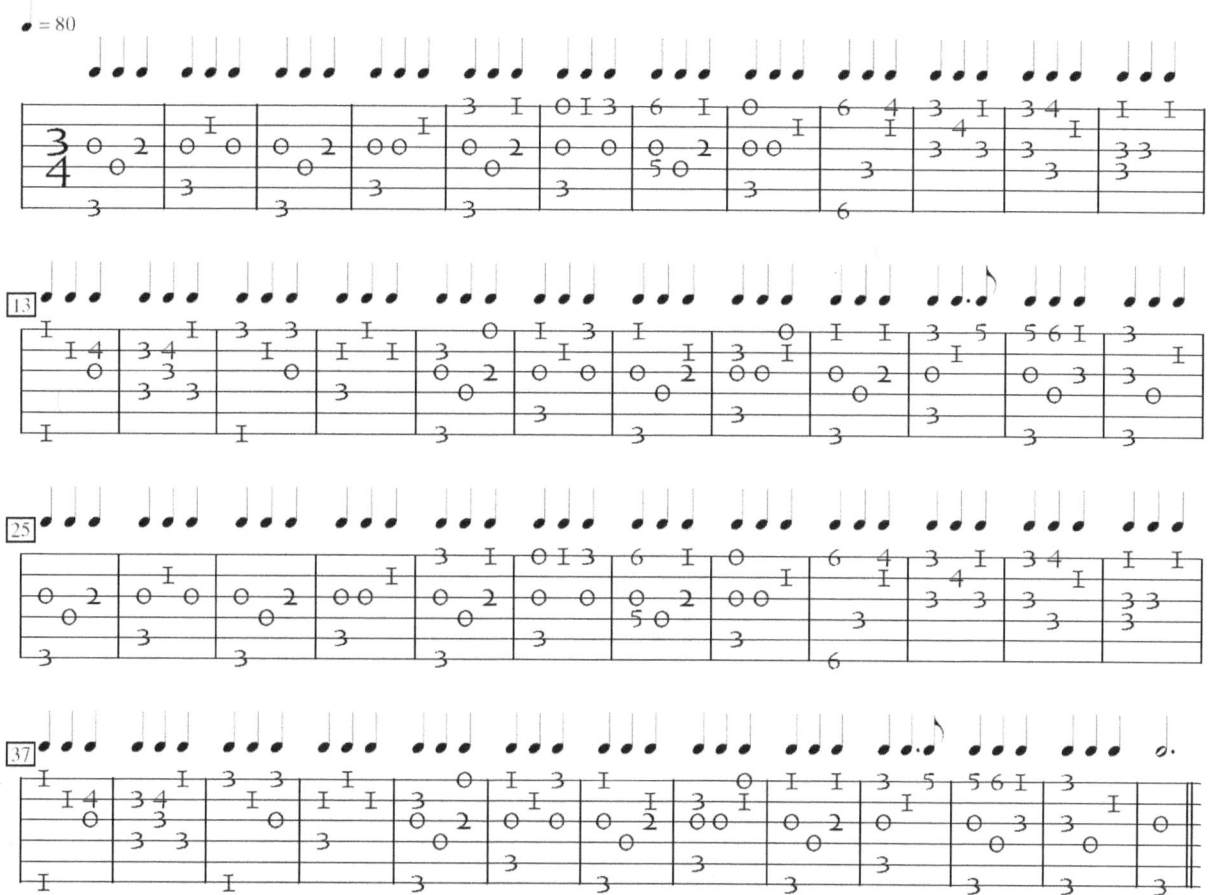

www.ingramcontent.com/pod-product-compliance
Lightning Source LLC
Chambersburg PA
CBHW051430070526
44584CB00023B/3669